STATES

IDAHO

A MyReportLinks.com Book

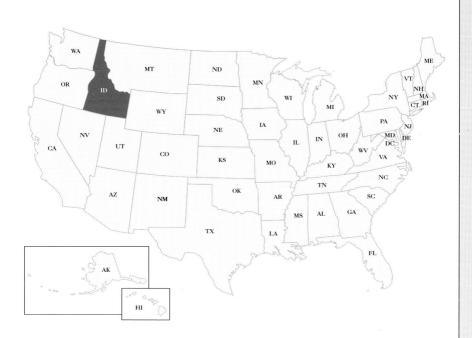

David Schaffer

MyReportLinks.com Books

an imprint of

 Enslow Publishers, Inc.

Box 398, 40 Industrial Road
Berkeley Heights, NJ 07922
USA

To Idahoan Michael Simpson, simply and mindfully.

MyReportLinks.com Books, an imprint of Enslow Publishers, Inc. MyReportLinks is a trademark of Enslow Publishers, Inc.

Library of Congress Cataloging-in-Publication Data

Schaffer, David.
  Idaho / David Schaffer.
    p. cm. — (States)
  Summary: Discusses the land and climate, economy, government, and history of the Spud State. Includes Internet links to Web sites related to Idaho.
  Includes bibliographical references (p.) and index.
  ISBN 0-7660-5134-X
  1. Idaho—Juvenile literature. [1. Idaho.] I. Title. II. States
(Series : Berkeley Heights, N.J.)
  F746.3 .S33 2003
  979.6—dc21
                    2002153556

Printed in the United States of America

10 9 8 7 6 5 4 3 2 1

To Our Readers:
Through the purchase of this book, you and your library gain access to the Report Links that specifically back up this book.
The Publisher will provide access to the Report Links that back up this book and will keep these Report Links up to date on **www.myreportlinks.com** for three years from the book's first publication date.
We have done our best to make sure all Internet addresses in this book were active and appropriate when we went to press. However, the author and the Publisher have no control over, and assume no liability for, the material available on those Internet sites or on other Web sites they may link to.
The usage of the MyReportLinks.com Books Web site is subject to the terms and conditions stated on the Usage Policy Statement on **www.myreportlinks.com**.
A password may be required to access the Report Links that back up this book. The password is found on the bottom of page 4 of this book.
Any comments or suggestions can be sent by e-mail to comments@myreportlinks.com or to the address on the back cover.

Photo Credits: © Corel Corporation, p. 3; © 1997 by Photo File, Inc., p. 20; Dictionary of American Portraits, Dover Publications Inc., © 1967, p. 14; Enslow Publishers, Inc., pp. 1, 22; Idaho Black History Museum, p. 42; Idaho Department of Commerce, p. 13; Idaho Potato Commission/State of Idaho, pp. 18, 30; Idaho Rivers United, p. 16; Idaho Travel Council, pp. 11, 24, 26, 28, 34, 39, 41, 45; Library of Congress, p. 37; MyReportLinks.com Books, p. 4; Nathan Bilow © 1998, p. 19; National Park Service, p. 25; PBS, p. 32; Robesus, Inc., p. 10.

Cover Photo: © 1995 PhotoDisc

Cover Description: The Sawtooth Mountain Range in Idaho

Tools

Search

Notes

Discuss

MyReportLinks.com Books

Go!

Contents

MyReportLinks.com Books
Great Books, Great Links, Great for Research!

MyReportLinks.com Books present the information you need to learn about your report subject. In addition, they show you where to go on the Internet for more information. The pre-evaluated Report Links that back up this book are kept up to date on **www.myreportlinks.com**. With the purchase of a MyReportLinks.com Books title, you and your library gain access to the Report Links that specifically back up that book. The Report Links save hours of research time and link to dozens—even hundreds—of Web sites, source documents, and photos related to your report topic.

Please see "To Our Readers" on the Copyright page for important information about this book, the MyReportLinks.com Books Web site, and the Report Links that back up this book.

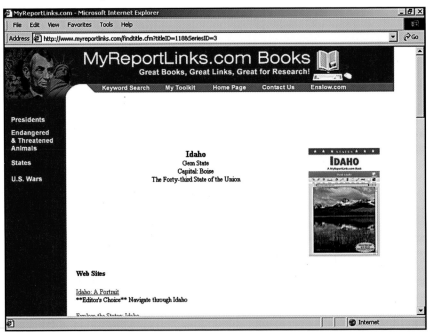

Access:

The Publisher will provide access to the Report Links that back up this book and will try to keep these Report Links up to date on our Web site for three years from the book's first publication date. Please enter **SID7254** if asked for a password.

Tools   Search   Notes   Discuss   Go!

Report Links

↗ The Internet sites described below can be accessed at
http://www.myreportlinks.com

*EDITOR'S CHOICE

▶ **Idaho: A Portrait**
This PBS Web site explores many aspects of the state, including its
history, geology, and people. You will also find maps and photographs.

Link to this Internet site from http://www.myreportlinks.com
*EDITOR'S CHOICE

▶ **Explore the States: Idaho**
America's Story from America's Library, a Library of Congress Web site,
tells the story of Idaho. Here you will learn interesting facts about the
state and about mountains that look like a saw!

Link to this Internet site from http://www.myreportlinks.com
*EDITOR'S CHOICE

▶ *World Almanac for Kids Online*: **Idaho**
The *World Almanac for Kids Online* provides essential information
about Idaho. Here you will learn about land and resources, population,
education, economy, history, and much more.

Link to this Internet site from http://www.myreportlinks.com
*EDITOR'S CHOICE

▶ **Lewis and Clark in Idaho**
Set out on an adventure as you travel the Lewis and Clark Trail in
Idaho. View maps, read the biography of Sacagawea, and browse an
interactive map that presents points of interest on the trail.

Link to this Internet site from http://www.myreportlinks.com
*EDITOR'S CHOICE

▶ **U.S. Census Bureau: Idaho**
The U.S. Census Bureau Web site provides facts and figures about Idaho.
Here you will learn about the population, economy, and geography.

Link to this Internet site from http://www.myreportlinks.com
*EDITOR'S CHOICE

▶ **Perry-Castañeda Library Map Collection: Idaho Maps**
From the Perry-Castañeda Library Map Collection Web site you can
explore state, city, historical, and national park maps of Idaho.

Link to this Internet site from http://www.myreportlinks.com

Report Links

The Internet sites described below can be accessed at
http://www.myreportlinks.com

▶ All About Idaho: Women in Idaho History

Here you will find information about women in Idaho history. Included are biographies on such women as Emma Green, designer of the Idaho State Seal, and Sacagawea, the Shoshoni member of the Lewis and Clark expedition.

Link to this Internet site from http://www.myreportlinks.com

▶ American Park Network: Mount Rushmore History

Did you know that Idaho born Gutzon Borglum was a student of the great French artist Auguste Rodin? Learn about the Mount Rushmore National Memorial, one of America's most treasured landmarks, and its creator.

Link to this Internet site from http://www.myreportlinks.com

▶ Appaloosa Horse Club: Encyclopedia

Learn about Idaho's state horse, the Appaloosa. The site includes a photo gallery, history, and Hall of Fame information. Do you know what a pastern is? Look at the diagram of a horse and find out!

Link to this Internet site from http://www.myreportlinks.com

▶ Borah Peak

At this Web site you can learn all about Borah Peak, Idaho's largest peak. Here you can explore trails, photographs, and weather conditions.

Link to this Internet site from http://www.myreportlinks.com

▶ Coeur d'Alene Tribal Council

Learn about this Idaho American Indian tribe. See how their government works and learn about their ancestral lands. A few photos are also included. Read about the tribe's fight to gain environmental control of the Coeur d'Alene watershed.

Link to this Internet site from http://www.myreportlinks.com

▶ Craters of the Moon National Monument

From the National Park Service you can read information about how volcanism created the Craters of the Moon National Monument. Learn about the animals, plants, environmental factors, and natural features of this preserve. Photo gallery included.

Link to this Internet site from http://www.myreportlinks.com

Report Links

▶ **Dialogue for Kids**
At this Web site you will find facts about dams and learn about
specific dams in Idaho, such as the American Falls Dam, Minidoka
Dam, Dworshak Dam, and others.

Link to this Internet site from http://www.myreportlinks.com

▶ **Electrical Engineer: Philo Farnsworth**
Philo Farnsworth was raised in Rigby, Idaho, where he supposedly had
his first notion of electronic television. This article from *Time* magazine
recognizes Farnsworth as one of the Top 100 most influential people of
the twentieth century.

Link to this Internet site from http://www.myreportlinks.com

▶ **Famous American Trials: Bill Haywood Trial 1907**
Read this fascinating account of the trial of Bill Haywood, the man
accused of ordering the assassination of former Idaho governor Frank
Steunenberg. Included are biographies, maps, testimony, and images.

Link to this Internet site from http://www.myreportlinks.com

▶ **Famous Idaho Potatoes**
Idaho is known for its potatoes, and at the Famous Idaho Potatoes
Web site you will learn why. You will also learn nutritional facts
about potatoes, recipes, and tips on cooking potatoes.

Link to this Internet site from http://www.myreportlinks.com

▶ **The Governor of the State of Idaho: Dirk Kempthorne**
Learn about the current and past governors of the state of Idaho. Also
included on this site is a time line of the history of the state and the
state seal, song, and symbols. A virtual tour of the state capitol is
also presented.

Link to this Internet site from http://www.myreportlinks.com

▶ **Hagerman Fossil Beds National Monument**
At this National Park Service Web site you will learn what a Hagerman
horse is. You will find information regarding other fossils found in the
Hagerman Fossil Beds. Also included is a geology section that gives
information on various areas of Idaho.

Link to this Internet site from http://www.myreportlinks.com

 The Internet sites described below can be accessed at
http://www.myreportlinks.com

▶**Idaho Black History Museum**
Visit the Idaho Black History Museum Web site. Here you will find
information about the civil rights movement. Read along and find
out what happened and when.

Link to this Internet site from http://www.myreportlinks.com

▶**Idaho Bureau of Land Management**
The Idaho Bureau of Land Management Web site offers information about
wildlife, plant life, recreation, forests, and much more. You will also find an
index of interesting places in Idaho, such as Craters of the Moon National
Monument and Snake River Birds of Prey National Conservation Area.

Link to this Internet site from http://www.myreportlinks.com

▶**The Idaho Historic Preservation Council**
Read how the Idaho Historic Preservation Council is working towards
preserving historical landmarks in Idaho. View photos, and learn about
the ten most endangered historical places.

Link to this Internet site from http://www.myreportlinks.com

▶**Idaho Museum of Natural History: Digital Atlas of Idaho**
Learn about the geology, biology, archaeology, geography, hydrology, and
climatology of Idaho. The site includes written descriptions of Idaho's
natural history, photographs, maps, sounds, and glossaries.

Link to this Internet site from http://www.myreportlinks.com

▶**Idaho Rivers United**
Here you will find statistics and information about the rivers of Idaho. See
what is being done to preserve these natural resources. In the 'Protect Idaho
Rivers' section you can view photos and read about each river and its issues.

Link to this Internet site from http://www.myreportlinks.com

▶**National Register of Historic Places: Idaho**
This site lists historic places in Idaho by county. You will get information
about each site, including historic significance, architecture style, period,
and more. A map of Idaho showing each county is also included.

Link to this Internet site from http://www.myreportlinks.com

The Internet sites described below can be accessed at
http://www.myreportlinks.com

▶**Nez Percé Indians**
This PBS Web site provides a brief overview of the Nez Percé Indians.
Here you will learn about their culture, history, and how they assisted
Lewis and Clark's Corp of Discovery.

Link to this Internet site from http://www.myreportlinks.com

▶**The Official Walter Johnson Web site**
Read the biography of baseball great and native Idahoan Walter
"Big Train" Johnson. He was named one of the top athletes of the
twentieth century by ESPN.

Link to this Internet site from http://www.myreportlinks.com

▶**The Oregon Trail**
From the creators of the award-winning documentary "The Oregon
Trail," comes a site that includes the history of the trail, historic sites
along the trail, diaries, and books. Everything you ever wanted to know
about the famous trail can be found here.

Link to this Internet site from http://www.myreportlinks.com

▶**Randy Weaver: Siege at Ruby Ridge**
From the Crime Library Web site you can read an article about Randy
Weaver and the events that occurred at Ruby Ridge.

Link to this Internet site from http://www.myreportlinks.com

▶**University of Idaho Library: Kate and Sue McBeth**
Learn the history of the McBeth story through photos, personal letters,
and government documents. Old maps are presented, including one by
Kate McBeth, denoting Christian homes in the area.

Link to this Internet site from http://www.myreportlinks.com

▶**The West is Burning Up!**
From the Idaho Forest Web site you can learn about the fire of 1910.
Learn about the fire that raged for almost a year and took the lives
of many.

Link to this Internet site from http://www.myreportlinks.com

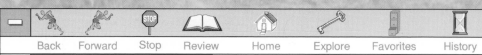
Capital
Boise

Counties
44

Population
1,293,953*

Gained Statehood
July 3, 1890, forty-third state

Bird
Mountain bluebird

Tree
Western white pine

Flower
White syringa

Horse
Appaloosa

Fish
Cutthroat trout

Gemstone
Star garnet

Fossil
Hagerman horse fossil

Vegetable
Potato

Nickname
Gem State

Song
"Here We Have Idaho" (by Bethel Packenham, McKinley Helm, and Sallie Hume-Douglas)

Motto
Esto perpetua
(Let it be perpetual)

Flag
The state seal sits in the center of the flag. It consists of a woman holding the scales of justice, a miner, an elk's head, mountains, a pine forest, and harvested grain. The state motto is printed in a banner across the top, and the seal is surrounded by a yellow frame with the words "Great Seal of the State of Idaho" printed on it. The seal is set against a blue background with "State of Idaho" printed below it in yellow letters on a red background. A yellow frame borders the flag on three sides.

Population reflects the 2000 census.

The State of Idaho

The state of Idaho lies in the mountainous Northwestern United States. It ranks thirty-ninth among the states in population, with just under 1.3 million people. Idaho covers over 83,574 square miles, placing it fourteenth among the states in area.

Because its land is mostly rugged and remote, Idaho has been lightly settled for most of its history. However, the state experienced rapid growth during the late twentieth century. In the 1990s, the state of Idaho was the

▲ Hells Canyon National Recreation Area, established on December 31, 1975, is North America's deepest river gorge. The remote, 650,000-acre area straddles the borders of western Idaho and northeastern Oregon. It includes almost nine hundred miles of trails.

fourth-fastest growing state with an increase of over 28 percent in its population.

▷ Early Settlers and Explorers

American Indians arrived in Idaho about 14,500 years ago. The Shoshone and Bannock Indians, who mostly lived in the south, and the Nez Percé, who lived in the north, were two large tribes that frequently battled each other. Other tribes with significant numbers of people in Idaho were the Paiute and Bannock in the south and the Coeur d'Alene, Kootenai, and Pend d'Oreille in the north.

The American Indians in Idaho played an important role in helping Meriwether Lewis and William Clark, the first white people to explore the area. Lewis and Clark were sent by President Thomas Jefferson to explore the vast Western territories the United States purchased from France in 1803. During their passage through Idaho, the explorers received aid from a Shoshone woman named Sacagawea. She helped Lewis and Clark successfully pass through extremely difficult terrain, and also helped them trade with the Lemhi Shoshone Indians of the area.

Due to the reports of Lewis and Clark, word spread about the great opportunities for fur hunting and trapping in Idaho. This brought many new people into the area. Over fifty thousand people passed through Idaho during the mid-nineteenth century. Most followed the Oregon Trail, a passageway that lead from Independence, Missouri, to the northwest Pacific coast. More people came to Idaho after gold and silver were discovered there in the late nineteenth century, and Idaho became a United States territory in 1863. With an increasing presence of white people in Idaho came tensions and conflicts with American Indians. The whites settled on land the

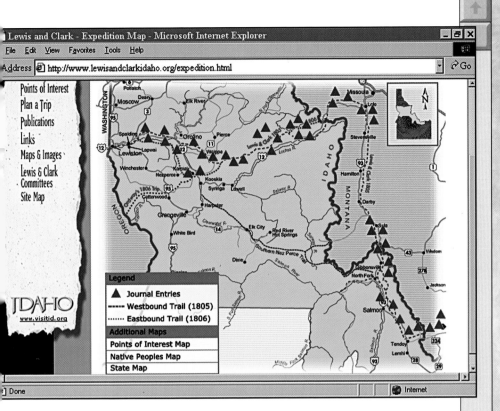

Lewis and Clark - Expedition Map - Microsoft Internet Explorer

File Edit View Favorites Tools Help

Address http://www.lewisandclarkidaho.org/expedition.html   Go

Points of Interest
Plan a Trip
Publications
Links
Maps & Images
Lewis & Clark
Committees
Site Map

IDAHO
www.visitid.org

Legend

▲ Journal Entries
----- Westbound Trail (1805)
······ Eastbound Trail (1806)

Additional Maps
Points of Interest Map
Native Peoples Map
State Map

Done   Internet

▲ *Meriwether Lewis and William Clark traveled westward across Idaho in 1805, as well as during their return trip home in 1806.*

American Indians considered their own. Often the whites treated the land in ways the natives regarded as disrespectful. The whites also sought to drive the American Indians from their homeland and relocate them to reservations. The American Indians resisted, leading to fierce battles with United States soldiers.

▶ Conflict and Conquest

The Bear River Massacre of 1863 was the bloodiest slaughter of American Indians by government forces in United States history. Almost four hundred of the northwestern band of the Shoshone, including many

women and children, were killed. Decisive battles between whites and American Indians in Idaho took place in the Nez Percé War of 1877. One Nez Percé leader was Chief Joseph. He tried to lead his people north to safety in Canada when he realized that the forces opposing the Nez Percé were too powerful for them to overcome. About forty miles from the border, Joseph and the Nez Percé were stopped by the military. Exhausted by a journey in which they had fled 1,500 miles and lost about half of the eight hundred people they had started with, the Nez Percé surrendered. Chief Joseph turned over his rifle and made a speech that gained lasting fame:

> I am tired of fighting. Our chiefs are killed. . . . The old men are all dead. . . . It is cold. . . . The little children are freezing to death. My people, some of them, have run away to the hills . . . I want to have time to look for my children. . . . Hear me, my chiefs: My heart is sick and sad. From where the sun now stands, I will fight no more forever.[1]

A couple of brief wars followed, but the Nez Percé surrender is regarded as the end of serious American Indian opposition to white control of Idaho.

▶ Statehood and the Modern Age

It was not until railroads were built in Idaho that large-scale, permanent settlement developed. The first rail

◀ *Chief Joseph.*

Tools   Search   Notes   Discuss   Go!

line in the state linked Pocatello, in southeastern Idaho, with Salt Lake City, Utah, and Butte, Montana, in 1869. Tracks reaching across the country were built in the 1880s after the discovery of major silver deposits in Idaho. Silver required more machinery and equipment to mine and transport than gold, so the silver discoveries led to much greater development in the state. This substantial growth helped Idaho to enter the Union as the forty-third state in 1890.

Growth in Idaho was also fueled by major irrigation late in the nineteenth and early in the twentieth centuries. Canals and dams built on Idaho's major rivers helped turn large areas of desert into fertile farmland. Rivers and dams were also important in providing a source of hydroelectric energy to the state. Idaho has many large dams that contribute to both farming and power generation. These include Arrowrock Dam on the Boise River and American Falls Dam on the Snake River.

Idahoans have become more concerned about their natural resources and environment. During the 1950s and 1960s, dams were built that did not allow the passage of fish. This badly hurt Idaho's salmon, which had provided plentiful fishing since the time of the American Indians. Another great environmental concern is pollution caused by nuclear power generators. The Idaho National Engineering and Environmental Laboratory was opened in 1949. Important breakthroughs in the creation of nuclear energy are made at the laboratory, but it also creates concerns about nuclear waste and contamination.

Identifying Features

Idaho has vast and plentiful mountain ranges, forests, and waterways. Their natural beauty, wildlife, and the

Idaho Rivers United - Save Salmon and Steelhead - Microsoft Internet Explorer

File Edit View Favorites Tools Help

Address http://www.idahorivers.org/salhome.htm

Save Salmon and Steelhead
RESTORING IDAHO'S WILD, OCEAN-GOING FISH

The Incredible Journey

return to last page

IDAHO RIVERS
U N I T E D

Protect Idaho's Rivers
Save Salmon and Steelhead
• Salmon News
• Information
• action
• Salmon Links
Support Idaho Rivers United
River Activism
Media
River Store
About Idaho

Biologists estimate that when Lewis & Clark passed through Idaho on their way to the Pacific in 1805, Idaho's rivers and streams teemed with 4 million wild salmon and steelhead.

When Lewis and Clark passed through Idaho on their way to the Pacific in 1805, biologists estimate Idaho's rivers and streams supported 4 million wild salmon and steelhead (ocean-going rainbow trout).

The mighty Snake, Salmon and Clearwater rivers produced some of the greatest chinook

Internet

▲ *Approximately 4 million wild salmon and steelhead swam Idaho's rivers when Lewis and Clark passed through the state in 1805. Now these fish are on the brink of extinction.*

recreational opportunities they provide have become what many people associate with Idaho. The attraction of nature is well demonstrated by the Sun Valley Resort located in south-central Idaho. This resort enjoyed immediate success even though it was built during the Great Depression of the 1930s. Railroad executive Averell Harriman wanted to build a first-class ski resort somewhere in the Western United States. He hired an expert skier, Austrian Count Felix Schaffgotsch, to look for a good location to build the resort. A site near the old mining town of Ketchum was chosen. Schaffgotsch wrote to Harriman after viewing the area: "Among the many attractive spots I have visited, this combines more delightful features than any place I have seen in the United States, Switzerland, or Austria for a winter sports resort."[2] This favorable reaction has been shared by many other visitors to Sun Valley, including celebrities and political leaders from around the world.

Many other outdoor activities are available in Idaho. The Salmon River offers some of the best whitewater rafting in the world. Deer, elk, and moose are some of the game sought by hunters and nature lovers alike. With millions of acres of preserved wilderness, there are plenty of opportunities for camping, fishing, and hiking.

Potato Supreme

Probably the one thing most people identify with Idaho is the potato. Indeed Idaho produces more potatoes than any other place in the United States. In 2001, the state's potato production totaled about six thousand tons. Most Idaho potatoes are used for making frozen products and french fries, but fresh whole Idaho spuds are also a popular grocery item.

Famous and Important Idahoans

The potato business has produced well-known Idaho businessmen. Two brothers, Nephi and Golden Grigg, founded the Ore-Ida company. It was the first producer of commercial, frozen french fries and potato nuggets, and remains a leading frozen food maker. John Richard Simplot gained a fortune by selling packaged, dried potatoes to the army during World War II. In 1957, he began selling frozen fries to McDonald's, the world's largest restaurant chain.

▲ *Spuddy Buddy is the cartoon icon for Idaho's potato industry.*

In national government, Idaho has had two senators who have gained prominence on issues of nature conservation and foreign policy. William E. Borah was elected to the U.S. Senate in 1906 and served thirty-four years. Frank Church, elected in 1962, served in the Senate until 1980. The Frank Church River of No Return Wilderness Area was named in his honor in 1984.

Cecil Andrus, governor of Idaho from 1971 to 1977 and again from 1987 to 1995, also served as secretary of the interior under President Jimmy Carter. Andrus played a major role in creating two major national recreation areas in Idaho in the 1970s.

Some famous writers, actors, and artists have lived in Idaho. Ezra Pound is one of the most acclaimed poets of the twentieth century. Born in Hailey, Idaho, in 1885, Pound moved away with his family at the age of two. Another literary giant, Ernest Hemingway, lived in Idaho at the end of his life. Hemingway had a vacation home in Ketchum, Idaho, for nearly twenty years before settling there. He died in Idaho in 1961. Lana Turner became a legendary movie figure in the 1930s. She was born in the town of Wallace, Idaho, in 1920 and was discovered at a soda counter in Hollywood when she was fifteen years old. Sculptor Gutzon Borglum, born in Idaho in 1867, was commissioned to carve the faces on Mount Rushmore in South Dakota in the 1920s and 1930s.

△ *Picabo Street was born on April 3, 1971, in Triumph, Idaho. In 1995, Street became the first American skier to win the World Cup down-hill championship.*

Walter Johnson was born in Kansas, but grew up in Idaho.

Some famous athletes have been either born or raised in Idaho. Pitcher Walter Johnson and power hitter Harmon Killebrew are both members of baseball's Hall of Fame. Rigby, Idaho, native Larry Wilson played football for the St. Louis Cardinals as a defensive back. He was selected for both the Pro Football Hall of Fame and the All-Millennium Team. Perhaps the most famous sports star who is a lifelong resident of Idaho is downhill skier Picabo Street. Named for a small Idaho town near her birthplace, she started skiing at Sun Valley as a child. Street came to worldwide attention when she won medals at the 1994 and 1998 Winter Olympic Games and the 1995 World Cup.

Land and Climate

Idaho borders the Canadian province of British Columbia on its north side. Montana and Wyoming lie to the east, Utah to the southeast, and Nevada to the southwest. To the west, Idaho is bounded by Oregon and Washington. The variety of Idaho's landscape and climate is wide. Several mountains in Idaho tower more than ten thousand feet above sea level, but Idaho also has places with elevations more than one thousand feet below sea level.

Idaho is an oddly shaped state. It has been described as resembling a frying pan. On its northern border, Idaho is only 45 miles from east to west, but in the south it is as wide as 285 miles. From north to south, Idaho is 486 miles long in the west, but only 175 miles long in the eastern part of the state. This unusual shape is due to a history of changing boundaries during the nineteenth century.

▶ Land of Contrasts

The dramatic differences in elevation within Idaho can be seen at Hells Canyon, located along the Oregon border. This is the deepest river canyon in North America. Its average depth is over five thousand feet and at its deepest point it is eight thousand feet.

Climate also varies greatly within Idaho. The record high temperature in the state is 118°F, while the record low is −60°F. Temperatures statewide average 23°F in winter and 67°F in summer, but there are big differences between mountains and low-lying areas. In the higher

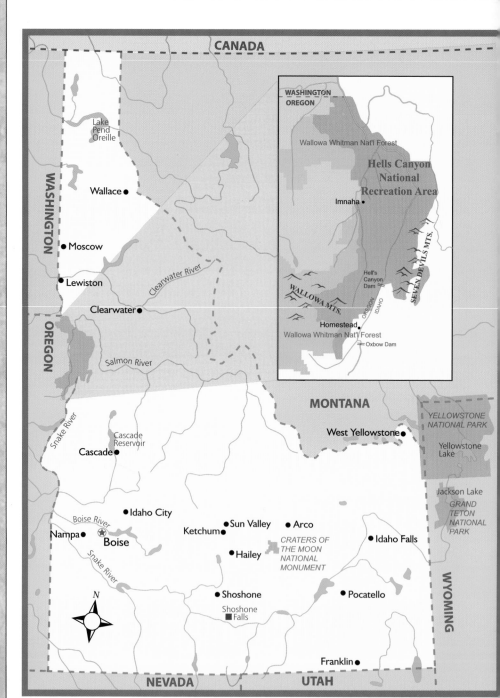

▲ A map of Idaho and Hells Canyon.

elevations, winter lows average below 20°F, while in the southwest they average in the mid-twenties. Summer highs average over 90°F in the southwest, but only in the low eighties in the higher elevations.

There are also big differences in rain and snowfall levels. The south gets about thirteen inches of rain per year, while the north gets thirty inches. While the southwest gets only about 20 inches of snow per year, mountainous areas of the state receive anywhere from 70 to 120 inches.

Outstanding Geological Features

At 12,662 feet, Mount Borah is Idaho's highest point. Three other Idaho peaks also rise over twelve thousand feet. The lowest elevation in the state is found along the Snake River, Idaho's longest river, which winds for 1,038 miles. The river's source on the eastern border is over 7,000 feet above sea level, while Lewiston, on the Clearwater River in Idaho, is just 710 feet.

The Snake River is Idaho's most important waterway, and the river valley is the state's major residential and business area. When pioneers passed through Idaho in the nineteenth century on the Oregon Trail, they were discouraged from settling along the Snake. Historian F. Ross Peterson explains why: "The Snake River was never viewed as a friendly stream. . . . It was difficult to cross and the canyons in many areas are so deep that the water was always near, yet inaccessible. . . . When the Oregon-bound pioneers viewed this impassable canyon, they left the Snake and headed west."[1]

The Snake River valley is mostly arid desert. It was only through irrigation that its fields and pastures have turned so productive. Other major rivers include the Salmon, located in central Idaho and named for the fish

that live in abundant numbers in its water, and the Clearwater, located in the north.

Idaho has many large lakes. The largest is Lake Pend Oreille, which is located in the narrow, northern area known as the panhandle. It measures 180 square miles.

Idaho has some other unique geological features. Craters of the Moon National Monument is so named because its landscape resembles the surface of the moon. The area actually has been used to train astronauts to walk on the moon. The strange landscape was created by lava flows that occurred about fifteen thousand years ago. Ancient lava flows also affect the course of two rivers, the Big Lost River and the Little Lost River. Both rivers get "lost" in sponge-like lava deposits and filter into an

▲ The Snake River makes up the northern portion of the Idaho-Oregon border. Also, 67.5 miles of the river carve through Hells Canyon, creating the deepest river gorge on the continent.

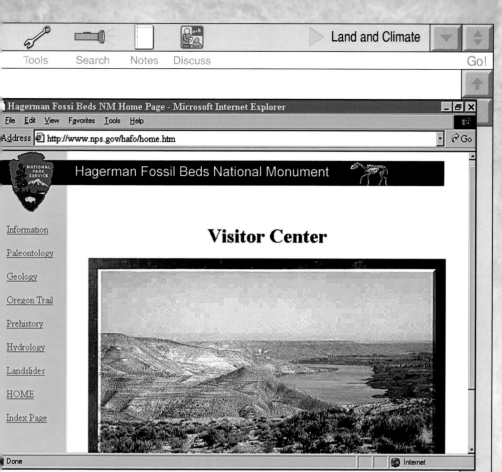

Hagerman Fossil Beds NM Home Page - Microsoft Internet Explorer

File Edit View Favorites Tools Help

Address 🕮 http://www.nps.gov/hafo/home.htm   ⟳ Go

Hagerman Fossil Beds National Monument

Information
Paleontology
Geology
Oregon Trail
Prehistory
Hydrology
Landslides
HOME
Index Page

Visitor Center

Done   🌐 Internet

🔺 *The largest concentration of Hagerman horse fossils can be found at Hagerman Fossil Beds National Monument, located in Hagerman, Idaho. The national monument protects the world's richest known fossil deposit, dating back 3.5 million years.*

underground reservoir. The water from the rivers resurfaces 120 miles away at the Thousand Springs in the Snake River valley. Shoshone Falls is sometimes called "the Niagara of the West." At 212 feet high, it is actually about 50 feet higher than the famous falls at Niagara.

▶ Regions and Major Cities

Idaho has four distinct geographic regions. The Northern Rockies take up most of the northern panhandle and central Idaho. The Columbia Plateau covers southwest Idaho

and also extends north into part of the panhandle. In the southeast are the Great Basin and the Middle Rockies.

The Northern Rockies and Columbia Plateau comprise over three-quarters of the state. The Northern Rockies include most of the state's highest mountains. Mining and lumber have been major industries in this area throughout Idaho's history. This is also the area where most of the state's recreational and wilderness areas are found. With about thirty-five thousand people, Coeur d'Alene is the largest town in this region. The Columbia Plateau is the state's most populated and developed region. It includes the state capital and largest city, Boise, which has about 185,000 people. The second largest city, Nampa, is located about twenty miles west of Boise. The northern river port city of Lewiston is also within the Columbia Plateau Region.

▲ *Boise is the state's largest city.*

The Great Basin, located in the southeastern part of Idaho sometimes is called the Fertile Crescent. The Snake River valley is not as arid here as it is further to the west, due to higher elevations and more precipitation. The cities of Pocatello and Idaho Falls, both with populations of over fifty thousand people, are located in this region. The Middle Rockies lay along the eastern border with Wyoming. The westernmost part of Yellowstone National Park lies within this region of Idaho.

Land Management and Preservation

Over 40 percent of Idaho's land is classified as national forest, meaning the federal government owns and controls that land. There is more national forest land in Idaho than in any other state except Alaska.

Land in a national forest is preserved and protected in its natural form unless the federal government approves other uses. There have been conflicts between those who wanted to maintain the natural state of these lands and those who wanted to use them for commercial purposes, especially the logging and mining industries. These conflicts have sometimes caused serious problems. Early in the twentieth century, people opposed to closing off such large areas of land from development kept the U.S. Forest Service from receiving funds needed to manage the lands. This contributed to a major forest fire in Idaho in 1910. One newspaper read, "the worst-ever fire season . . . will likely always remain with the summer of 1910."[2] Millions of acres of forest were burned in Idaho that year.

The destructive fire in 1910 made Idahoans and people in other western states realize the importance of maintaining and managing their valuable natural resources.

Economy

Idaho's economy has grown and evolved. Mining and forestry are two important industries that have long existed in Idaho. Crop growing and raising livestock also became important early in Idaho's history. During the mid- and late-twentieth centuries, hydroelectric and nuclear power emerged as major industries in the state. Outdoor sports and recreation, especially skiing, became big businesses in Idaho during that time as well. Late in the twentieth century, high-tech and modern retail and tourist businesses gained a strong presence in Idaho, particularly in Boise and other larger cities.

◀ Skiing has become an important industry in Idaho's economy.

▶ Exploiting Nature's Bounty

The first westerners to make their livings in Idaho did so from the area's natural resources, often without caring about the long-term effects. Furs worn as outerwear were popular among wealthy Europeans early in the nineteenth century. The discovery of beaver, otter, and other furry animals in the Northwest led many to set up short-term settlements for the purpose of hunting and trapping. Those who pursued these animals lived a sparse and rugged existence and were known as mountain men. Later forts and trading posts were built along Lake Pend Oreille and the Snake River to support the fur trade. Competition for the available furs was tough. British and French-Canadian fur companies also hunted and trapped in the area. With so much hunting and trapping activity, populations of many furbearing animals were greatly reduced. Then, declining popularity of furs as fashion items also hurt the fur business in Idaho.

Gold discoveries in Idaho in the 1860s led to sudden and rapid growth. Lewiston was founded as a result of the gold rush, and for a while, Idaho City (with about six thousand people) was the largest city in the Northwest. These towns remained after the gold rush was over, but many people left when the gold was gone, leaving several ghost towns in the Sawtooth Mountain area of central Idaho.

Other minerals have proven to be of greater and longer-lasting importance to Idaho's economy. Two major silver discoveries in northern Idaho in 1885 led to the development of the mining industry in the area. Railroads were built to transport the silver ore. Unlike gold, silver needed to be melted down and smelted in order to be extracted. Idaho became, and continues to be, the largest silver producing state in the nation. Lead and zinc are other minerals produced from mines in northern Idaho. In the south there is significant mining of phosphorous, a mineral used in commercial fertilizers.

The two major lumbering and wood production companies in Idaho are "Boise" and "Potlatch Corporation." Both companies started early in the twentieth century.

Their success is due largely to the replacement and control of the amount of wood they cut down. Currently there are serious conflicts between conservationists and major lumber companies over forestland use. Yet, for many years, Idaho has produced large quantities of wood while also protecting and caring for its forests.

Sowing the Seeds of Farming

Agriculture is a thriving industry in Idaho, due largely to ambitious irrigation efforts beginning at the end of the nineteenth century. The Carey Act, passed in 1894, encouraged states to irrigate their barren lands. Ten years

▲ Idaho is the biggest potato-producing state in the nation. This is due to the state's natural climate, which provides the perfect conditions for potato farming.

later, over half the lands irrigated as a result of the act were located in Idaho.

Potatoes were already being grown in Idaho before these large irrigation projects. However, with vast new lands now available for planting, the state's potato output rose more than thirty-fold during the first three decades of the twentieth century. Historian Leonard J. Arrington explains why Idaho potatoes are so popular:

> Idaho's growing conditions and growers simply produce a superior variety. Potatoes grow well in high altitudes where the growing season is warm and sunny in the day and cool at night, where the soil contains a high level of moisture (regulated by growers with irrigation), and where the soil is light like the volcanic ash in Idaho's potato growing areas.[1]

Besides potatoes, Idaho also produces large amounts of grains, hay, peas, and sugar beets. Cattle and sheep herding contribute significantly to Idaho's agricultural economy. Sheep herding is especially suited to the state's mountain pastures. One group of people who has come to Idaho in large numbers since 1890 to raise sheep are Basques, an ethnic group from Spain. Sheep herding is a traditional trade among Basques. So many have come and stayed that Idaho now has the largest Basque population in the world outside of Spain.

Education

Idaho's businesses are supported by a diverse state-sponsored university system. One of the largest schools in the state is the University of Idaho in the northern city of Moscow. It would be expected that the university has high quality agricultural and forestry programs, but it also is strong in engineering and science. Idaho State University

in Pocatello began as a technical college and is still strong in technical training as well as medical fields. Boise State University, located in the capital city, offers programs in liberal and fine arts, business, engineering, and music.

Modern Idaho

Both hydroelectric and nuclear power have been important to Idaho. The first hydroelectric power in the state was generated by Swan Falls, located on the Snake River. Several other dams help create hydroelectric power, including three in Hells Canyon and the Dworshak Dam in northern Idaho. The Idaho National Engineering and Environmental Laboratory, located west of Idaho Falls, is

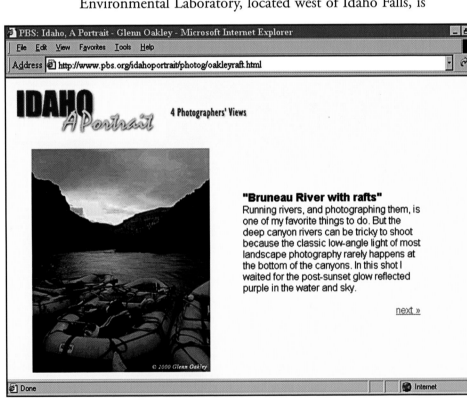

PBS: Idaho, A Portrait - Glenn Oakley - Microsoft Internet Explorer

File   Edit   View   Favorites   Tools   Help

Address http://www.pbs.org/idahoportrait/photog/oakleyraft.html

IDAHO *A Portrait*   4 Photographers' Views

"Bruneau River with rafts"
Running rivers, and photographing them, is one of my favorite things to do. But the deep canyon rivers can be tricky to shoot because the classic low-angle light of most landscape photography rarely happens at the bottom of the canyons. In this shot I waited for the post-sunset glow reflected purple in the water and sky.

next »

© 2000 Glenn Oakley

Done   Internet

▲ *Idaho's Snake River and the Middle Fork and Main Salmon rivers are popular rafting spots.*

a major nuclear power facility. The plant began providing nuclear energy for public use at the laboratory in 1951. The nearby town of Arco became the first place in the world to be powered entirely by nuclear energy on July 17, 1955. Power from the laboratory provided Arco's electricity for one hour.

Skiing and other outdoor sports have made tourism a lucrative industry for the state. Aside from Sun Valley, other ski resorts include Schweitzer Mountain in the north, Pebble Creek in the southeast, and Bogus Basin in the southwest. Many other fun and exciting activities are available in Idaho. Boating and fishing in the Frank Church River of No Return Wilderness Area and Hells Canyon National Recreation Area create millions of dollars for the state's economy every year. Two ice caves in south-central Idaho, Shoshone and Crystal, are also popular tourist spots. Massacre Rocks State Park preserves a historic section of the Oregon Trail.

Computer and electronics products and services have become a prominent part of Idaho's economy. Hewlett-Packard and Micron, two major global high-tech companies, employ thousands of Idahoans. Along with other young professionals, high-tech workers have helped make Boise into a hip, modern urban center. The city's downtown area features streets lined with cafes, shops, and galleries geared toward the young and stylish. With large numbers of people coming from major cities to Idaho, modern businesses and urban culture will likely continue to undergo strong growth in the state.

Chapter 4

Government

For much of Idaho's history the state government has had to deal with a highly divided population. There have been divisions among the state's people based on economic class, race, region, and religion. These have presented great challenges to those who lead the state.

▷ Government Structure and Organization

Idaho's state government still functions under the state's first constitution. It was adopted in 1889, and has been amended over one hundred times. Like most states and

△ Construction on Idaho's capitol building, located in the state capital of Boise, began in 1906 and ended in 1912. The east and west wings were added between 1919 and 1920.

the United States federal government, Idaho's government has three branches: executive, legislative, and judicial.

The executive branch includes the governor, lieutenant governor, attorney general, secretary of state, controller, treasurer, and superintendent of public education, who are elected for four-year terms. No one may be elected for more than two consecutive terms.

The legislature has a house of representatives, and a senate. Thirty-five districts in the state elect one senator and two representatives every two years.

The judicial branch is headed by the Idaho Supreme Court. This court has five justices, each elected for a six-year term. Justices on the court elect a chief justice to serve for a four-year term. Below the supreme court is a court of appeals with three justices serving six-year terms. There are seven district courts located throughout the state.

There are also important government positions on the county level. Every county in Idaho has a board of three elected commissioners. The offices of sheriff, tax assessor, prosecuting attorney, coroner, treasurer/tax collector, and district court clerk/auditor/recorder are also decided in elections at the county level. Every county also has at least one local court.

Conflict and Crisis

Some people in Idaho have often felt more like a part of another state or territory. The northern panhandle is part of the Spokane, Washington, metropolitan area. The earliest settlers in the southeast came from Utah, and people there felt closely connected to Salt Lake City. Even in the southwest, where the state's capital and the largest portion of the population live, there are strong ties to Oregon.

Regional divisions were one reason that Idaho's government was in chaos during its territorial period. Another reason is that, at first, the federal government appointed Idaho's governors—the people had no voice in the selection. Many Idahoans thought the federal government showed no care or consideration for them. F. Ross Peterson describes the situation in *Idaho: A Bicentennial History:*

> Sixteen different men were appointed governor, twelve actually served, but six of the twelve spent less than a year in the area. . . . However, all of Idaho's territorial problems . . . were often blamed on these [outsider] governors. Accused by Idahoans of corruption, fraud, theft, speculation, and conflict of interest, the governors rarely remained in office for their full four-year terms. At times the allegations were true.[1]

The governor's office continued to be troubled after Idaho gained statehood. In 1892 and again in 1899, there were violent clashes between miners and owners. After the mining companies cut workers' pay or fired them for trying to organize unions, pro-union workers wreaked havoc on major company facilities, including mines, processing plants, and office buildings. After such incidents the governor had to ask for federal troops to come in and restore order. The governor during the incident in 1899 was Frank Steunenberg. After his term ended he was murdered outside his home. Many people believe his murder was committed by a person or group who resented his strong crackdown against union actions.

▷ Outstanding Contributions

During the 1910s, Idaho's elected officials made significant achievements and gained recognition. Moses Alexander became the first Jewish governor in the United

States in 1915. Senator William Borah rose to national prominence because of his great speaking ability and his strong advocacy of natural preservation. What probably earned Borah his greatest fame was his opposition to the United States joining the League of Nations, an international organization created after World War I to keep world peace. C. Ben Ross was governor during the Great Depression. He took bold measures to help relieve Idaho's economic problems. These included enacting controversial tax laws.

▲ William E. Borah (left) was a notable attorney prior to his term as a Republican senator from Idaho. Here he converses with Hiram Johnson, a senator from California.

Two late-twentieth century government figures, Senator Frank Church and Governor Cecil Andrus, became involved in a conflict with a major mining company in the 1970s. The American Smelting and Refining Company wanted to extract minerals from a large area in central Idaho, using open-pit techniques. This is a form of mining that is particularly damaging to the land and surrounding environment.

Working together, Church and Andrus got two new national recreation areas created that put the lands the mining companies wanted off limits. Church previously had gained prominence by being an early opponent of United States military actions in Vietnam.

During the late-twentieth century two Idaho women, Gracie Bowers Pfost and Helen Chenoweth, were elected to the U.S. House of Representatives. Pfost served for ten years in the 1950s and 1960s; Chenoweth from 1995 to 2001.

History

In its early days, Idaho was very much a Western frontier state. Pioneers, gold rush settlements, and American Indian wars played major roles in the state's history. While Idaho is still largely wilderness and geographically remote, it is now a modern, growing state with a hopeful future.

▶ Idaho's First Residents

American Indians in Idaho lived a nomadic or semi-nomadic lifestyle. Tribes depended more on hunting and gathering for their existence than they did on farming.

△ *This image of a lake in the White Cloud Mountains shows that some areas of Idaho still appear much as they did hundreds of years ago.*

There was rivalry between the Nez Percé in the north and the Shoshones and Bannocks in the south. Although, these tribes also sometimes traded and interacted peacefully with each other.

The American Indians in Idaho were strongly affected by white people even before the whites came to the area. This was because horses, introduced to western American Indians by the Spanish, made their way north to Idaho early in the eighteenth century. This made travel much faster and easier. Different tribes and factions came into closer contact with each other. For instance, the widespread use of horses led to an annual event held in Treasure Valley in southwest Idaho. American Indians would come from many different tribes and great distances to trade, gamble, and dance. White fur traders who came to Idaho in the nineteenth century continued the gatherings, calling them "rendezvous."

The Creation of Idaho

The exploration by Lewis and Clark of the territories obtained by the United States in the Louisiana Purchase was of great importance to the development of the Western frontier. In his book *Idaho*, author John Gottberg says that "there is little doubt that it was the last of the contiguous forty-eight states [all the states except Alaska and Hawaii] to be seen by European-American eyes."[1] Following the Lewis and Clark expedition there would be further exploration by whites in Idaho. Gold seekers built homes, forts, and towns. However, for more than half a century, most settlement in Idaho was temporary.

The first people to create long-term settlements and establish lasting communities in the state were Mormons from Utah. Mormon is another term for a member of the

△ *The Lewis and Clark National Historic Trail is a total of 3,700 miles long. It begins in Illinois, and winds through Missouri, Kansas, Iowa, Nebraska, South Dakota, North Dakota, Montana, Idaho, Oregon, and Washington.*

Church of Jesus Christ of Latter-day Saints. Franklin in the southeast, located just north of the Utah border, became Idaho's first permanent settlement in 1860. More Mormons moved into southeastern Idaho during the 1860s. In contrast to the fur and gold seekers elsewhere in the state, these settlers built towns and villages that remained.

▷ **Discord and Dispute Among Idahoans**

Mormons became unpopular in Idaho as the territory grew larger and gained statehood. Dislike of Mormons stemmed mostly from their custom of allowing men to have more than one wife. However, even after this

practice was outlawed by the federal government in the 1860s, anti-Mormonism remained strong in Idaho. For a time, Idaho residents could be prevented from voting if they did not take an oath swearing they did not belong to the Church of Jesus Christ of Latter-day Saints.

A number of factors helped encourage migration to and settlement of Idaho late in the nineteenth century. One factor was the end of American Indian resistance by the 1880s. The discovery of additional minerals besides gold, as well as irrigation in the dry valleys of southern Idaho, led to construction of roads and railway lines and

▲ *The Idaho Black History Museum, located in Boise, was established in 1995 to help educate the public about the struggles of African Americans in United States history with a focus on those events that occurred in Idaho.*

the building of new towns and cities. It became easier for people to reach Idaho from greater distances, and a smaller proportion of new residents came from nearby Utah. By the time Idaho became a state in 1890, the Mormons were still a significant part of Idaho's population but had become a minority.

During the gold rush years of 1848 to 1860, many Chinese came to Idaho. By 1870, they comprised half of all the miners in Idaho and nearly one third of the territory's total population. Some people saw the Chinese as intruders, and resented the success of these newcomers. There was prejudice and even violence against the Chinese. Over one hundred Asians were killed in beatings and attacks in the late 1860s. People of Asian descent faced discrimination again during World War II. Japanese people throughout the country, especially in the West, were forced to live in internment camps after Japanese forces attacked Pearl Harbor on December 7, 1941. One of these camps was built in Mindoka, Idaho. It housed about ten thousand people at one time, and was the major Japanese detention camp in the Northwest.

▷ Facing Natural and Human Adversities

Besides the massive forest fire of 1910, Idaho has faced other catastrophes of natural and human cause. In 1976, the Teton Dam burst and flooded the Teton River valley. There were eleven deaths and thousands of homes were destroyed. In October 1983, an earthquake measuring 7.3 on the Richter scale hit the state. It killed two children and caused millions of dollars worth of damage.

Idaho's wilderness and remoteness has sometimes attracted anti-government militants who claim they are independent from the United States. Perhaps the most

notorious event to occur in Idaho in recent years was the incident known as Ruby Ridge. In 1992, Randy Weaver and his family, who held radical views regarding religion and government, came to national attention. When Weaver was charged with illegally trafficking in firearms in the summer of 1992, he refused to cooperate with police. Federal law agents surrounded the Weaver mountain cabin for eleven days. Before the standoff was resolved a gun battle resulted in the deaths of Weaver's wife and son and a federal agent. The incident came to be known as Ruby Ridge, the name of the mountain area where the Weavers lived.

Ultimately even many people who opposed the Weavers questioned the government's handling of the case. Many people thought the government might have been too aggressive and contributed to the tragic deaths.

▷ Idaho Grows in Size and Importance

After becoming a state, Idaho's population grew dramatically. About one hundred thousand people lived in Idaho in 1890. That number had tripled by 1910. The growth and development of the state enabled it to make a significant contribution to the nation during World War I. Idaho's farms, forests, and mines increased production to meet the wartime demand, and the state prospered financially. The following decades were not as good.

During the 1920s, crop prices dropped sharply, causing hardship among farmers. Much of the money that agricultural and other businesses had borrowed could not be paid back. For Idahoans, the Great Depression of the 1930s actually started in the 1920s. On the other hand, toward the end of the 1930s, Idaho's economy began to recover sooner than most other states. A large influx of

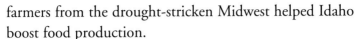

farmers from the drought-stricken Midwest helped Idaho boost food production.

Idaho's governor, C. Ben Ross, worked with President Franklin D. Roosevelt on the New Deal policies that most benefited the state. The New Deal was Roosevelt's plan for pulling the country out of the Depression. One New Deal program that especially helped Idaho was the Civilian Conservation Corps. The Corps ran seventy mountain camps in Idaho that employed over eighteen thousand people on construction and forest restoration projects.

Following World War II, there were many signs of economic growth. Idaho emerged as the nation's leading potato producer in the 1940s. The state's progress in hydroelectric and nuclear power became increasingly important in a world seeking energy sources. The forests and mountains of Idaho were well suited to serve the demand for outdoor sports and recreation, which also rose greatly during the twentieth century.

A thorough look at Idaho shows that there is much to admire and celebrate about the state.

It is easy to understand ▶ why, in 1997, 32 percent of out-of-state visitors came to Idaho to visit attractions or natural areas.

Chapter Notes

Chapter 1. The State of Idaho

1. Chief Joseph, quoted in John Gottberg, *Idaho* (Oakland, Calif.: Compass American Guides/Fodor's, 2001), p. 51.

2. Count Felix Schaffgotsch, quoted in Dorice Taylor, *Sun Valley* (Sun Valley, Idaho.: Ex Libris, 1980), p. 23.

Chapter 2. Land and Climate

1. F. Ross Peterson, *Idaho: A Bicentennial History* (New York: W. W. Norton & Co., 1976), pp. 7–8.

2. Tom Grote, "The Big Blowup," *The Idaho Statesman,* August 19, 1979, p. 26.

Chapter 3. Economy

1. Leonard J. Arrington, *History of Idaho Volume I* (Moscow: University of Idaho Press, 1994), p. 487.

Chapter 4. Government

1. F. Ross Peterson, *Idaho: A Bicentennial History* (New York: W. W. Norton & Co., 1976), p. 92.

Chapter 5. History

1. John Gottberg, *Idaho* (Oakland, Calif.: Compass American Guides/Fodor's, 2001), p. 38.

Further Reading

Faber, Harold. *Lewis and Clark: From Ocean to Ocean.* Tarrytown, N.Y.: Marshall Cavendish, 2002.

Fisher, Ronald K. *Beyond the Rockies: A Narrative History of Idaho.* Coeur d'Alene, Idaho: Alpha Omega, 1993.

Fradin, Dennis Brindell. *Idaho.* Danbury, Conn.: Children's Press, 1998.

George, Charles and Linda. *Idaho. America the Beautiful Series.* Danbury, Conn.: Children's Press, 2000.

Kummer, Patricia. *Idaho.* Mankato, Minn.: Capstone Press, 1998.

Lied, Kate. *Potato: A Tale from the Great Depression.* Washington, DC: National Geographic Society, 1997.

Stefoff, Rebecca. *Idaho.* Celebrate the States Series. Tarrytown, N.Y.: Benchmark Books/Marshall Cavendish, 2000.

Taylor, Marion W. *Chief Joseph: Nez Percé Leader.* Broomall, Penn.: Chelsea House, 1993.

Thompson, Kathleen. *Idaho. Portrait of America Series.* Austin, Tex.: Raintree Steck-Vaughn Publishers, 1996.

Wadsworth, Ginger. *River Discoveries.* Watertown, Mass.: Charlesbridge Publishing, Inc., 2002.

Young, Virgil M. *Story of Idaho: Centennial Edition.* Moscow: University of Idaho Press, 1990.

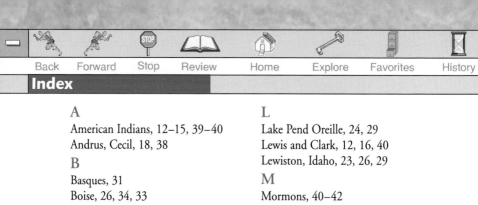